Anxious
Latitudes

Wesleyan New Poets

Anxious
Latitudes

Ralph Angel

Wesleyan University Press ⬡ Middletown, Connecticut

The American Poetry Review: "History," "Breaking the Rock Down," "Pas de Deux," "Arm and Arm," "Ground Glass," "Home Poem"; *Green House:* "As It Is"; *New Orleans Review:* "Fragile Hardware"; *Partisan Review:* "Falling Behind," "Not to Reach Great Heights, But to Stay Out of Great Valleys," "Anxious Latitudes"; *Ploughshares:* "You Are the Place You Cannot Move," "Committing Sideways"; *Quarry West:* "Transient News," "The Bread," "Recurring Motel," "Tatters"; *William and Mary Review:* "Untitled." The poems "Between Two Tracks" and "Cyclone Off the Coast" appeared originally in *The New Yorker.* "Back Down" originally appeared in *Poetry East #15,* Fall, 1984. "Home Poem" also appeared in the *Anthology of Magazine Verse & Yearbook of American Poetry 1984.* The poem "History" was originally published as a chapbook by Atticus Press.

This book is supported by a grant from the National Endowment for the Arts.

LIBRARY OF CONGRESS CATALOGING IN PUBLICATION DATA
Angel, Ralph, 1951–
    Anxious latitudes.
    (Wesleyan new poets)
    I. Title.
PS3551.N457A59   1986   811'.54   84-19711
ISBN 0-8195-2124-8
ISBN 0-8195-1125-0 (pbk.)

All inquiries and permissions requests should be addressed to the Publisher, Wesleyan University Press, 110 Mt. Vernon Street, Middletown, Connecticut 06457

Distributed by Harper & Row Publishers, Keystone Industrial Park, Scranton, Pennsylvania 18512

Manufactured in the United States of America

First Edition
Wesleyan New Poets

In memory of
Hanula Bendicha Angel
and Isaac Nahmias

Contents

1

History

The engines' eternal rumbling. I never get used to it.
Night smoke. Steel dust. The sickly
sawww and *sskreee* of wheels holding the rail.

Never get used to rigid awake, throatful
of ashes and oil. Tons of knuckle. Tons of tightening
slack. Of erosion, impact, tons of freight car.

Never the yard light, wax of formaldehyde.
Never the switch list in the eye's spittle.
Never a charred nerve

that drifts from the cold forest of thinking.
Thinking that a man's five impossible senses
can be that far away.

2

A night wears on, but grows no older.
And a man, a man lights a cigarette
and walks on dirt and thinks he is building

a train. We know the task so well that
knowledge is a blindfold, and for every
thrown switch and passed signal,

for each load of lumber and coal, fuselage
and tank, the routine proceeds no further
than loneliness. So many hours

after school, gathering flat stones and pieces of
dull glass, sending them skipping over
dusk on the lake. The mute chorus

of tree bark and twigs, feathers, the twitching
reeds in the shorewater. It's not just the renewal
but the way these mounds of spilled

wheat and sugar, etched with rat tracks, are drawn
into the strange mutterings of men walking toward death.
A single, empty cattle car on the bend—

the smell of shit and straw, the horribly
normal expressions of human beings
reduced to animal heart and animal bone

because there's a history too large,
because there are men who think they write the story.
And we go on interrupting a life that's out of our hands.

A man bashes a 2-×-4 to splinters on the side of a boxcar.
He lines up pennies on the track so that the wheels might
smear them into something new.

3

Slowly, methodically,
clanking and bumping over the switches,
a long drag is pulled out toward the main.

Forty, maybe sixty cars,
and the last unfolds the whole of the north end.
Out of emptiness, a cat's squeal

and the cat scrambling across the tracks.
A newspaper lifts up, and touches back.
Shreds of cloth on a broken post.

A moth, dizzy and circling.
And an old guy, coughing, stumbling out of some bushes.
He watches an owl scissor past the tower.

He looks down to twisted cable and busted cans,
to a crumpled shoe as pale as dirt.
He shoves his hand in his pocket, and looks over at me.

You Are the Place You Cannot Move

You wake up healthy
but you don't feel right. Now everything's
backwards and you're thinking of someone to blame.

And you do, you're lucky,
drinking coffee was easy, the traffic's
moving along, you're like
everyone else just trying to get through the day
and the place you're dreaming of seems possible—
somewhere to get to.

All you really know
is that it hurts here, the way feelings
are bigger than we are, and a woman's face
in a third-story window, her limp hair
and pots of red geraniums luring you
into her suffering until you're walking on roads
inscribed in your own body. The maps
you never speak of. Intersections, train stations,
roadside benches, the names of places and
people you've known all bearing the weight
of cashing a check or your having to eat something,
of glimpsing the newspaper's ghoulish headlines.

Like everyone else, you think,
the struggle is toward a better time, though
no pressure surrounds the house you were born in.
Cool, quieter, a vast primitive light
where nothing happens but the sound
of your sole self breathing.
And you've decisions to make—isn't that why
you've come?—with a baldheaded man at the bar
and your friends all over the place, anxious,
tired, a little less sturdy than you'd hoped for
and needing someone to kick around, someone to love.

Man in a Window

I don't know   man   trust is a precious thing
a kind of humility   Offer it to a snake and get repaid with
   humiliation

Luckily   friends rally to my spiritual defense
I think they're reminding me

I mean it's important to me   it's
important to me   so I leave my fate to fate and come back
I come back home   We need so much less   always   always
and what's important is always ours

I mean I want to dedicate my life to those who keep going
   just to see how it isn't ending

I don't know
Another average day
Got up   putzed around 'til noon
took a shower and second-guessed myself   and
all those people   all those people passing through my
my days and nights   and all those people   and
and you just can't stay with it   you know what I mean
You can't   can't stay with it   Things happen
Things happen   Doubt sets in   Doubt sets in   and
I took a shower about noon   you know   and I shaved and
thought about not shaving but I
shaved   I took a shower and had a lot of work to do but I
I didn't want to do it   I was second-guessing myself   that's when
   doubt got involved

I struck up a
rapport with doubt   I didn't do any work   and so
and so I said to myself   I said   well

maybe I should talk about something– but I didn't learn
    anything
I couldn't talk about anything– there was
lots of distraction today
A beautiful day   Lots of distraction   It had to do with
all these people– all these too-many people
passing through my days and nights   But I
don't get to hear about ideas anymore– know what I mean
Just for the hell of it   Talking about ideas
Takes the mind one step further
further than what it already knows   Doesn't
need to affirm itself   It's one step beyond affirming itself

Vulnerable– in a way that doesn't threaten
even weak people   Those nice-guy routines
They come up to you
because they know how to be a nice guy

Breaking the Rock Down

Now that we've finally arrived here
you won't let me hold you.
And were you stopped along the way by a reason to believe,
you've escaped with it and made thinkable
that web of incomplete darkness, crawling with
rumors on a far side of evening.

So the menus are left unopened.
Business as usual. I heard nothing, nothing
about *you*, though this time some shard of
ricocheting gossip will have an effect—
it will hurt somebody. Will you avoid that too?

If we could just get back here
we'd hardly notice the music and
voices that slip in from the bar, the ground fog
rising to the height of the city.
And for all the vicious man-made shoving
we are angry spectators craving admirers
when we bet the farm on selfish confusion, as if time were
an accident, dragging it all down to rock
and breaking the rock down.

It's okay to feel afraid. It must be.
But what seeks your measure in the eyes of
other survivors? You're seized again,
and again fighting back, again fighting unfairly,
expecting each pool of resilience to contain you
and to judge you. When someone reacts
you think you are winning, that winners possess more.

And the truth, the truth stays with the resemblance
but honesty, forgive me, grows tired
and it takes what I know about myself
and leaves the way I came—alone.
And now you are telling me how much you need me,
need my friendship, but what about
who it is you are?

Committing Sideways

This might hurt a bit, stabbing away at conversation
when we could be quiet or snoring, I mean
waking up sick is tomorrow's business (we like to say
that it wears our clothes). But what's substantial
is the soulful intersection of the needs and obligations
of good friends ridiculing each other. It's a chance

we don't hesitate to take, and we're a shambles,
aren't we? These arms don't work anymore. Better stack them
over here, where the suntans fell off our faces. And yes,
that's the old philodendron walking out in your slippers,
but forget it, it's nothing, the whole place and its aura
of lived-in azaleas are resting on tentative sand.

Funny little murmurs of free fall. Now we're
getting somewhere, so close and, therefore, so disappointed,
like slaphappy derelicts leaning on parking meters
after the shoppers have thinned away, and yet from them
emanates an excited kind of trust that can also turn inside out
and make visible what has remained so secret.

And we each say, "Well, here's to you, bub," as the last
jokes collide with the things we most
despise in ourselves, which march across the table like crummy
peanut-butter sandwiches in Day-Glo trench coats—whoops,
there they go—right through the breathy curtains,
right past the worry that we may be anything but

deadly serious when they return to us, as they always do,
when we're alone, and that our having to think about them
will hold us too safe and too separate, our feet
squarely planted in dreaded plots of ground.

Falling Behind

Falling behind, I was trying to hold on
to a stray branch stuck in the grass, a crowd of
bathrobes in a driveway, a missing gatepost
to alter the day, making it bearable. But as I drew closer
their difference loosely spread
through neutral streets, grey autumn, the way
ground fog or sadness gathers this city—
cold around the edges seeping in like rain through sleep.

People go on. Countless footsteps
pass through car doors, wind up stairs and arrive
at far corners right on time. The victories there:
conversation. The calm strangers. The most available identity.
I couldn't know what doesn't change must be done
over and over again. I was thinking hard, chipping away
at my heart, unattaching a string of
birds from the wires, and disregarding them.
Each sound and nerve end
gives in to the dull sirens supporting the distance,
sounds in a memory without the memory's story.
The sighing, indecisive breeze
accumulates in the grave that was opened the day I was born.

Fir trees wander through the afternoon.
I was catching up with myself. Here's the newspaper,
the packets of Kasseri and Feta.
There's the drugstore's clean tile, the J & M cardroom,
the butcher's red flag. I was watching the woman
who snagged her sweater on the table.
I wanted to leave. I was already letting go.

Transient News

Well, fidgeting strangely, I woke up.
You see, I spent the night with Laura
because Laura's husband was out looking
for Laura. Toast and melon—she
poured the coffee, and I had to tell her
that I dreamed I was Ricky Ricardo.
"Some things they just go down
that way," she said, "even in America."

By then, I knew the tourists
had infiltrated Jackie's Odds & Ends.
Copped the newspaper. Tried to coerce
an aged couple into spotting me twenty
for showing them the brighter side
of their quarrel. The gentleman half
flinched his eyebrows and dreamed
he was the pubescent child in the candy aisle.
I was transferring items
from my left to my right rear pocket.
What can a poor fool do? Join
the Air Force? Wage war in Omaha?
This is a lovely town all right, like
a postcard, but you can't look at it forever.

I don't know. I should still
feel proud of myself, cordial, a regular
businessman during the eviction hearings.
Me and the landlord, we struck a deal.
Bitter? Nah, even left a lamb chop
on the cooler, and when the landlord
thought to call for keys, I took the time
to send them. Weeks later,

he lost the building.
Flies live there now.

Well, we could wait all afternoon for the bus,
and I think we have. The guy on the bench
straightens his nylons before striking
a melancholy pose. The lawyer
used to be a priest, the nurse has been married
five times, and the baker, he secretly
hates sugar. So I turn again
to the schoolgirl. She's so fat and pretty and shy,
and seems so fatalistic. I don't know,
but as I squeeze through to the back
of the bus, it's the whole tragedy
of everything being so unchangeable
and tired.

Afterward, We May Want to Know What Happened

Amazing. We're all still here,
and everybody's talking at once.
But each moment works against us—we can't
hear everything—and gets us through the hour
in buses and taxis, airplanes
carving the sky, the slow shade of a cloud
that creeps through an open market with promises of
nighttime striking a deal with the daylight.

No. We can't see everything,
but when did looking convince us?
Now we don't want these flowers,
and we curse the vendor for showing them.
It's all regret, the fish on the ice,
the baskets of potatoes and green beans, all
regret, until regret too

is demolished. From the dust and rabble
steel skeletons stand in the grandeur of distance
and glass skin. And today, again,
we've hurried to Century City, but we arrive
forever early, unable to live up to our destination—
neither shades nor galoshes, but
the myth of afternoon.

Perhaps that's enough. Perhaps
it's all true. These designs of ourselves, and the wind,
somewhere else. Among corporate towers
and modular dunes, among vacant, dazzling plazas
we're all just here, and each voice
is a tiny fissure in the earth's veneer.
And each voice calls to us, calls in the spirit of
a beggar with something to give.

A Change in the Order

I remember distinctly
my own infancy, clearly as a photograph
or an old woman's story, or the rain-drenched interiors
of my body. And yet we rise each morning
and begin from scratch, as the desert
rises beneath the city—sand specks
in our coffee.

On the streets of my world
the sound of the engine,
of birds and footsteps and fragmented voices
streaming toward uneven horizons.
All the people I don't see
fall into me and become the same person,
each object, every other object,
and the hillsides vibrate the sound.

But what I pick out, and what selects me,
means more, the way
powers of the universe are concentrated
into tiny gestures. A shaft of light. A broom
leaning in a doorway, supporting
the entire tenement. Everywhere I go,
the same tension, the same incredible
basket of oranges. I can't say
how the butcher's hands have come to be so raw,
or why I'm trying to make them familiar
like some vein or tendon of memory, but
if I don't keep myself from letting them in
then I'm not even out here taking a walk.

Among the blurred pedestrians, the perspiring
mailman, the woman who can't hide
behind bags of tortillas—

I owe them their freedom. Even as friends
come to me for shelter, they are stronger
and healthier when they leave.

It is now 10:30, 10:30 in the morning,
and it is twilight. In a pale school dress,
a dark-haired girl sits on a curb, arranging pieces of
glass in the palm of her hand.
I look directly at her.
At her side, a pair of rubber sandals.
A dog, prancing diagonally across the street.
Oak tree, and sycamore. A boy on a bicycle,
screaming by.

The Bread

"Yeah, I kinda like this
two-bit apartment. Hospital green.
Call it my little grave,
           heh-heh. I
                like, I mean
                what I like I like
     waking up in the morning. Just
          so amazing!
Know what I mean?   One minute it's all
           night under the covers
                    like dark meat
warm in the gravy and the next minute's
a cold shower, and me in the mirror, shaving.
         Saturday? Well,
         if you say so.   Still,
      there is the awful business of
           unemployment.   Think I'll just
   arrange my cigarettes.   Only
          13½ low-tar Merits but
exactly 2 Winstons. 2 terrific
         Lucky Strikes alongside
         2 Salems
in the Salem package. Over there, on top, are a couple of
         my oldest possessions.
The plaster bird won by Aunt Roshalda
      in carnival singing contest: age 5.
           And this is my chunk
of diatomaceous earth. I like
                to remember
I found it east of the petrified forest.
            Ho God! The
severed foot, with the shoe still on, flies
   over a passing vehicle   and out of
                  TV
        camera

range.
　　　　　　　Then a park report: the new
poop-scooper law. Five dog
　　　　　　　s leashed to
　　　　　　　woman of starched-hair persuasion. An old
guy, baggy-pantsed, approaches and
　　　　　　　points, says　　　'It's
　　　　　　　people like you
　　who
　　　　　　　make this city a cesspool.'
'You kiddin,' she
retorts. 'When
　　　　　　was the last time you
　　　　　　　took a bath, Mac?'
'It's not me
　　　who stinks,
　　　　　　　lady, you
　　damn
　　　　idiot.'
Enough, already.
　　　　　　　You
　　　　　believe that trash?
Before breakfast? Here, have
a glass of orange juice.　　　　I call this
　　　　　　bent-up hanger
　　　　　　　my toaster. A slice
　　of bread here, balance
　　　　　like so, fire
　　　　the hot plate and *voilà*: in a few
minutes, toast!
　　　　See what I mean? It's
　　　　　　just the bread,
　　　　　　just the bread
　　　　　　　that's important."

Fragile Hardware

Phone call . . . stacks of something
on top and in the drawers of all the desks . . .
I think a thing done is a similar time of day, and all day long
the sun rattles our fragile hardware.
In the heart of the city, the window glare that becomes
each building is a door, and that door is closing.

I wanted romance to be a start. Right here, in the harsh open.
We show up for work, grow tired, isn't that
enough? Eye liner, the silken ties, we were making things easier,
and walking down Grand Ave. or drinking coffee at Pasquini's
we want to hear about so-and-so, who did such and such,
who did it again.

Rustling time like this, sharing a little necessary
agitation. Now let's mess up the surface,
knock a few colors around, avoid the scene of which we're
so obviously a part. Yeah you've heard my complaints before.
    You didn't think it could be done.
Do I understand your question?

So much you already know . . .
No one was for extravagance, but getting by
has come to feed us, and it puts us to bed.
In Pershing Square, a man falls to his knees
for all the wrong reasons. Outside the bank, a woman pulls
her fingers through her hair. She pulls harder.

Laugh Joker Laugh

You're right, it's complicated, but everybody
learns how to hide to survive.
Everybody damages the flesh, soars
like spirit, descends the black lake of his heart.
So many things are accomplished there. Tigers on fire,
the movement of stars.

Like anxious guests
in an unearned castle, it's so easy to overstay,
easy to lie through the teeth of a postcard,
to carve alibis from the washed-out distance of phone booths.
Convince one person that you're not doing any,
and you're not doing any. And convince me
that what you did do last night was important,
how it reminded you of '67 or '71 or '78,
how bad you were. Convince me
that you're a little down today, that it's all right,
you've turned a corner. There's just no end to all this,
the universe. But now and then you can get off.

If I don't tell you that I believe you,
or that your message is like a junkie's
translucent skin, it's because you're desperate for comfort,
and guilt is nothing but calculated,
cold-blooded emotion. There are times
when we stand in for one another, when we walk with people
at the bottom of the river and they're still crying mercy.

When you finally take yourself for granted,
I can trust myself trusting you.

I mean we might be Martians,
but that's better than feeling like Martians.
And sure, why not? Let's go, but
wait a minute, I mean you said it best,
"These two fleas decide to go
uptown, and one flea says to the other,
'Do you wanna walk or should we take a dog?'"

Between Two Tracks

Between two tracks of boxcars, closeness
is a clear eye, far from the crushed stones
that admit to nothing, maintaining a railroad.
They're all empties, doors open, and to look into one
introduces a confusion that lingers
and becomes another part of the protected space.
Warm hands in warm pockets.

At the waterfront the tracks are clearer.
Everything is twilight. The blue, flecked metal
illuminates the threads of my overalls. I want to ask
of the outstretched rails, of the utility poles,
their slow fan over Washington Street, Marion Street.
But their decisions have already been made.

The yellow blear of a taxi. Its wind lifting
the particular debris of our happiness:
playing card, paper cup, fake eyelash
trailing cool shadows to the water.
The zillion bubbles singing,
filtering upward like ghosts of flowers
that bloom on the slanted surface and stop singing.

Until pointless, I imagine I can go on
hearing them, calmly, up Western Ave.
The crosswalk beneath the bridge is dark
before the darkness fills it. The faraway sounds
of old things loosening unease me
like reluctant portions of too much I have hidden
stirring in my thickest skin. In the doorway
of Bob's Corner Café I wonder how long
it will take to focus. I hear a cough

and the rasp of a lighter. Somebody laughing. The blur
of small talk. I think about my nerves,
the strangeness and predictability of not wanting
to die here with a Tuesday-night special: ox tails
and dry rice, dabbed with gravy.
The warm air, of detergent and grease. My favorite table.
My favorite dark corner.

2

Recurring Motel

Already, the tired shoulders of the sofa
are nervous and discover how sleep becomes
another dark moment. The last gleams
of your head-oil vanish through the dull
stains of other fevers. Even the headache,
that was born from the cry, breaks down;

and your heart fills with the tilted lampshade,
starched towels, and subterranean folk songs of
names engraved on the tables. There is a need
to protect yourself, to unfasten the cold and believe
you have taken the hardest road to this motel.
You think about rising up and falling to the bed,

and you forget. At your feet, a package of
cigarettes and a shirt with a butterfly collar
grow small. The thin light of morning pales
and flattens the windows. Outside, the finches
are shy, chirping.

By Degrees

Nothing moves easily
outside the swamp of daydream. Nobody dries off in time.
The cold digs in like unwelcome memory,
knee deep, with a club in its hand.

If there's really something to eat
let's put our cards on the table and be done with it.
The need that stays inside poisons the wilderness,
stirs my tar, and I'm out
trying to make miracles of anything that might happen.

If love can't be collision, then nothing
is forgiven, and we're just hanging around here
wasting our difference.

As It Is

There was a basket of fruit between us.
We lasted with the shade
at opposite ends of the picnic table.

What was passing on did not appear
to age the foliage of afternoon.
The wind combed the moist leaves.

We kept feeling our long breaths would take
root; not a wrinkle of pain on our faces.
There was nothing we wanted to say.

Light filtered through the upper clouds.
Houses on the far hill reflected
an arrangement of insects and birds.

There was a basket of fruit between us.
We lasted with the shade
at opposite ends of the picnic table.

Occasional children blushed, clinging
to the vines. Everywhere, ferns
and mosses absorbed the knocking of limbs.

We kept feeling our long breaths would take
root; not a wrinkle of pain on our faces.
There was nothing we wanted to say.

Untitled

for Rothko

Where the green landscape
naturally grows darker, out there,
near the orange building,
only the green is visible
in that orange space,
nothing but orange in that green.

    *

We might pass through
those edges of skylight at night
and welcome the vague
activity we catch up to—
always in motion,
in the process of leaving, and

leaving. Sometimes, when
I'm really old, the balcony
too is a dream. Storms
of surrounding shape
are afloat on the eye's ocean,
just this far from shore.

    *

Even the ugly spasms of
self-pity are lost
to the symmetry of distance.
In my coldest fire
of solitude, when all the world
is that horizon,

my heart unfolds a trail, splitting
the grey, icy soil
from the darker vault of echoes,

though nothing, nothing
that keeps me out and nothing that
I create, keeps me.

*

We dance through the hours. Your yellow
dress and my violet
breath whirling until, exhausted,
we sense the quiet sigh
in our bouquets of pale laughter.
And like the tiny

scar along the edge of your ear
that calls forth the pain
we never quite shared, being here
and the way in which
we're feeling here, require strangely
that we feel this way.

Pas de Deux

The connections never complicate. Never
will happiness be told; it wears down unnoticed.

Back out of the mirror, up the wild staircase
winter may butterfly, and my newly acquired past

in its time. Always, the right to a day
without name in the repertoire of

incessant sickness that gathers the birds' shadows
before the birds have risen. Who will be ready?

And don't answer that. My mind has grown cruel,
quiet, and I go on thinking. Woman,

you would be a fine mist curling
over the furrowed hillside, but your hands.

And I won't speak for the sudden farmhouse,
beautiful and ruined, the dense, green foliage

behind it, falling into ribbons of horizons.

Don't Bother Me, I Want to Help

Those lights, strung out through vague miles,
are their own referents, and mean nothing to me,
not even a shrug. Clearly, the city's no more
than the street I choose to sit with. So long
that after a while I can hardly see
the small cause
behind plate-glass windows, and each square of
pavement corrals a time to be alone. I trace
a shrewd, confused bark to the young dog
crouching in the lower, right-hand corner
of a photogenic history. I want to hang around.

He appears, with his shopping bag, from an alley.
He wears wraparound shades, heavy
with an Egyptian will to survive. Still,
some part of me suffers his urge
to slide downstream, riding the current
he knows too well. And still, there is no plan
for him: my old shoes, perhaps, my left foot
or my right foot. This matter is of little concern.
I sacrifice what I most need, embarrassed
to be a very tiny person
redirecting unopened space.

In the Only Neighborhood

When I'm another cup of coffee
Burning cigarette throat
Pacing wolf pacing in circles
Circles around the last
Square inch of living room I know
I will never be able
To inhabit

Mrs. Willet lumbers across her porch
Same dress black tam same sidereal length
And duration of each placed doily
Red berry white mouse display
For mockingbird hawk hoot owl

And when it's thrashing
Awaiting massive self
Sedation to sever the ribbon of wakefulness
To exhaustion severing the eyelids
Of the heart pleading for the ordinary
Daytime construction of another
One-more-time unexpected
Betrayal

Mrs. Willet leads nocturnal shadows
Stringless cello concerto fevered by the dying
Moon and draws her bow once more to the stars
Twice smiling at the dim glow of houses
Neighborhood– breathing
On twitching foundations

Yes   I am getting tired now   yes
Thank you Mrs. Willet
Good morning   Sleep well

Earl Never Loses

Each evening the oldest
cardplayer in the White Ace Hotel
deals poker
against a bottle of gin. His opponent,
his partner, burns holes through
his stomach and sends the red animal
scurrying. But Earl never loses.
Half shrugging, he piles the patriotic chips
on his side of the table, apologizing
to the losers—his old friend Bubba,
and Red-Eye, and Slim.

He delights in squashing
cigar butts in the tin plate of
diced meat and corn,
in getting so fired up
that he stumbles, slipping farther
from the roar and click of
night streets, receding
still inward upon his indolence,
fashioned by warm breathings of decay.
It's usually the black maid
who discovers him face-down
on the vinyl tablecloth, and she cradles
his colorless head
as she helps him to the cot.

But tonight, mysterious knuckles
rouse his eyelids.
Earl figures it is the knock
of a new, youthful challenger
though he's unable to conjure strength
in the tiniest of his drunk fingers.
Yellow, thick lamplight
burns his eyes with the ridiculous

smirk on the lip of his shot glass—
a dream of witnessing
his own sudden birth, shocking him
out of this life. And later,
another dream, a way of
cursing everything.

Long after the stranger has disappeared
down the hallway, Earl awakens, though
the knocking persists, rhythmically,
like a code to be broken.

Without looking at his cards, Earl knows
this is a hand to bluff with.
He closes his eyes, a signal he is not
at home, and smiles, holding his breath
until he is forgotten.

Arm and Arm

Even sleep seems to flatter you. The stupid,
rubbery arm and arm around the lake . . .

And moonlight
the forgiving touch to a night without moon
though you never had to telegraph
questions to get where you are,
a radiant face among cool pillows,
clean skin setting out over dark waters.

It's as if time has closed its doors
once and for all. Stars strung like Chinese lanterns.
Your boat watches effortlessly a party you arranged
on the jetty. A party, too close
to bother going to. It should come to you.
A violin threading a canyon.
It should greet you like the pretty so-and-so
who always owes you something that distinguishes
and prefers you through the warm spots and the cold.

But to be here is farther and deeper
into the murky origin of mediocrity,
the first inaudible songs of our destiny
in a forest of fallen branches
where the thickest water presses through
to a lake that swells inside you

and bursts onto the carved mirrors, wire-rimmed
spectacles, the seersucker suit and Panama hat
that will never save you, never.

A fine silt and skeletal leaves rising.

Not to Reach Great Heights,
But to Stay Out of Great Valleys

There's a wind in the leaves of the trees.
It's a river of bone chips and feathers.
And the visible stars, in their airy
chasms, are fishes. I am kissing fishes.

I'm on my way to your place.
Do you hear my footsteps on the stairs,
and feel my cold lips
on your cheek? I am saying, "Hello, friend."

A few neighbors huddle on the corners
with upturned collars and turned-out
pockets. The blue smell of metal and
night things—an old gal snoozes with cans,

a bearded boy embraces a telephone pole.
And they're shooting each other, again,
at Los Globos. Splinters of bone
fall from the window like fish scales.

The band of spectators rises ecstatically.
They're the cause of their own
good fortune, they believe, but the lie
is like the crime itself, with its excuses.

"Hello, friend," I am saying
on top of the hill. You are wearing

stockings and slippers and a few sweaters;
it's always so cozy in your kitchen.

Have the pipes finally choked?
The ceilings are leaking. The stairwell
and hallway are lined with cake pans;
there are puddles everywhere. A puddle of

light has formed beneath your door. Ah, good.
I want you to be there. Are you there?

Back Down

I don't want to end here,
my head turned interminably
toward white and black shadows
prolonged behind a veil of eucalyptus trees.
End here. Like an office desk
or file cabinets, or keeping my head in order to respond
properly to a memo.
Oh, to get out of bed
and wash, only to be dragged
back down by the hands of somebody else's ritual.
To kneel before a sour notion of older days.
To surrender. To make money.

I want to know what you're doing now,
whether the work is dull or if, at least,
it goes well. And I'm thinking
of a dress you might be wearing, your fragrant shoulders,
the solitary water of your ancient calm.
A calm deeper than grief or boredom, distracting
a soul uprooted, hour by hour,
from the living bone.
So call me.
And whatever you do,
don't call, don't test me, you can't win.
If something creaks in the hallway,
if something winces or cracks under pressure
it belongs to you, and all my sincerity
is a hostile afternoon.
Don't call me. There's a meeting at four,
a report to be memorized, the pipes
gurgle and hiss and sound too important,
and I want you to call me,
I need to try to answer—
half sitting, half standing in the way of my life.

3

Cyclone Off the Coast

It's not so much the heat from the sun
and colors flooding the weird, rickety horizon,
or the heat-warped air over limp flags and bright brick,
where an ordinary sigh breeds what's right,
while the hard-core are properly disposed of
on the far-reaching hills. Cut and dry. Summer
sunbelt. No, nothing moves, and when Mrs. Flannigan
sees her son splash into the back-yard fountain
she hears nothing. And the gardener,
Fletcher, palpates a burned forehead before clipping
the hedge his partner just finished.
And the clouds high, so high in the sky—
who can account for the day
they arrived here, and why they won't go away?

Nighttime comes, and for what? The wee hours?
Bits of steam oozing up from the ruined streets,
street cleaners and thumping wharf rats,
the well-lit places, the false drug
that can't help the night, though it repaints
the angular expressions of a dead decade;
and for the losers not even passing out assures sleep
when the hushed chill changes the guards,
when their eyes loosen the burden of remembering;
and the memory, like the pain that is our distance,
shrugs the dawn with excessive heat, latent
and inclined to be its own source—ready when you are—
ripping up trees and tearing out hair, leaping
from bridges: a house whirling, a man whistling
in the azygous muscle, the rumpled wind.

Only the Birds Should Bird

But all these cards and letters,
they never bother us. Just
mature jokes, a little laughin an scratchin
among pals. And the real stuff,
though abandoned at a dusty crossroads,
can be counted on.

It was a question of back and forth, of give
and take. Suitcase, toothbrush, T-shirts,
the way a guy simply loses at the end—
at either end. I could have
sworn I had my mack down. Everyone seemed
so amused, privy to what they imagined
this life to be, pie-eyed and punch-drunk,
the blah, confessional, choked-up ya-yas.
They had been itching to do it like that.
I was glad they could be comfortable.

Returning to Silverlake,
I found my address had been changed.
Took it for granted
that this was my apartment, though the view,
the faint light of the observatory
on a slant of familiar but invisible
hilltop, still surprises me.
What part was left behind this time?
I could thank those who understand,
who come back or hang on, but the waking
is too early now. Heave a pillow at
the window, punch out the toilet door,
bust up some breakfast just to get

in between, where two pieces of
desert are stitched together because a highway
once drove a spike through the bloodless

continuum. Is my appointment
at 7 or 7:15? Did I kiss her at the gate?
What's the new clanking?
It should be sorted out soon, the cars
and the drivers are so far away, even
the sagebrush is leaving.
And it just hurts more and more,
and it just means less and less
when it comes to saying good-bye.

Tatters

Sure, the need was simple
and the effort crowds the Silver Dragon piano bar.
We know how much of us is missing. We know the camaraderie
of surrender, upright in our chairs. "Well, friend,
the next life is not about to appear tonight
though it offers its usual promises in the tunes of that
piano, ice tumbling through sleeves of rose-colored glass,
our ideal voices, the pout she must have learned

in California. We might say it's every bit of 1:17 a.m."
These things happen. Toss an arm around the thick of it,
but what to do about this unabashed momentum?
At first it's easy: man with factory squint
kicks ass of man wearing a black shirt, and then is inclined
to punch his face in. Pick and choose, "Dust the sucker,"
the good, the merely ugly, that random
kitchen shatter, the whole gala hubba hubba

parading into the background. On the wall
hangs the old Chinese *lung*, another wingless power of the air.
Like the girl who scratches a thumbnail across
her slick, lamé blouse, the pulse of unspoken noises
still jockeys for favors. Sure, one decent grope deserves
the same in return, but the truth is too often frivolous.
"Anyways," he blusters, "Billy's gonna buys us a drink."
"Tell me. Tell yourself to me."

Ground Glass

We were going round and round
until it must be the day before
that passes through our understanding of
hazy skies in the apartment windows

across the alley. And the light recalls neighbors
fixing breakfast, rearranging furniture,
opening and closing doors to what we take
most for granted: where we are,

where food and a bed and some of
our friends are, the hum of the city
and the time, subliminal, moving away
from the two o'clock of this day.

So, we're off in that direction. There's
the one shoe out ahead, and the shoe
that lags behind us—even the pale
obscure details of commitment may be trusted.

(The veritable green clouds. A pigeon,
cooing the air conditioner. Pockets. Brief pause.
Side-glance. Those who, upon entering,
declare a stiff wind down the hallway.)

Yes, we might hold the comfort, but to know that
is to feel how much commitment can never be enough.
Nobody is hungry, and everyone sits
at the table; no meal has been prepared, though

the napkins are politely unraveled.
And again, the present arrives without form.

The gloom, which has crept in, stays,
while desire fills the spaces between you

and the rest, making them real obstacles.
Everything is out of reach, jabbing the center
with the intensity of a touched-off mob.
Protection watches over its own body:

some of this nervousness feels good, pumped-up,
backing you into the hidden red brick,
into the same old story you shout
from the shadows of too much. A few people

turn and look, though they may not
have heard you, their faces are clearer,
hard-edged. A child pulls at his mother's blue
jacket and bends over backwards, his mouth

wide open, his eyes in the vertical sky.
At the corner a man stumbles through the crowd,
pushing another man into somebody else.
They all apologize, but you can't help worrying

about that ancient woman leaning on the bus stop,
so undeniably calm. And it's all right,
the way it comes to be understood, walking
along the avenue, with the others, to a later hour.

Secretive, but Honest

And the clouds are calling,
calling out to the waves of wheat
that break over the clouds.
Always, there is a wooden fence.
Always, the small stones
like footprints,
like men who are lost,
men who know that they are lost.
The stones are a reminder,
though they too
are out of the picture.

*

It's not so easy to be born
right now. Cold season,
and the scarf is outside of me.
These boots are outside of me,
and all this breath, the heartaches,
dead squirrels.
All this breath. All the days and all
the nights endow each sublime object,
each source of new direction.
We can only want what we need,
each useless thing, each other life.
Another shadow on a dimly lit wall
buttering toast in the steam of his coffee.
Nothing is really where it is.

*

I confess to knowing the whereabouts
of what you want from me. You are so easily pleased,
but to please, unfortunately,

is not a young detective's responsibility.
Even as we are the guilty parties, I will not
accept that kind of power. Each forage
locates the same pale hands, choking
the victim's laughable,
his pitiful and his wide-eyed, his nearly dead.
It is time, I think,
to live up to the price we pay.

City Country

"There was something particularly
funny about this photograph, but I seem
to have misplaced it," he said, in the last
quarter hour of the week in which two years of
his life boiled down to a few, nasty cusswords
strung together in new patterns—brilliant, almost floral,
like the orangish-green wallpaper he grew up with.
You know, some roosters doting over
some chickens. Some eggs. Or fences.
"We got bigger," he said, over and over again.

"I'm going home now," he said,
where the freeway bends from west
to north to the building shapes in the pastel healing.
Yes. A little time to call his own—
billboard or play field—and the feeling seemed
awake forever. And the feeling worse
awakened the outstretched spirit
flung over those foothills like clouds along elegant,
rocky pathways to the only funeral in any town.
Yes. Window. And the window
is properly locked.

"I remember Larry," he said, "walking
through the yard, stopping before the pear tree
or willow. He climbed the thin branches
in the way we used to do it at dusk—
quietly, with the moist cold.
We would see the lake from there,
and the grey island that seemed to look back at us;
and we would find the blue from there,
and the blue gradations of green.
It wasn't giving up really. Nothing much changed.
We, mostly far away."

Home Poem

The night sends another wave of breeze
up the curve of our necks, down the streets
into places already darkened. Assured, in fashionable wraps,
we can feel it this time and know from somewhere
the firmness of crosswalks, traffic going
that way, parti-colored shops and huge buildings
jammed to the grid of the city. At 11th
& Santa Monica we call it stylish, though
we're not the more inventive for saying so.
Beneath the marquee we are suddenly beige
in the beige light, a little dumpier, close together.
With this quiet, how our faces grow louder
and vague. And nobody shudders;
we don't take the risk, or it passes like tickets
through a hole in a window. At whatever distance
we are the easy invitation, a steadiness in line,
strengthening our avoidance and the other times.
We chatter, comb our hair, puff a cigarette, involved
in the movement, yet we sense
the damp, echoing parking lot, the reach for our keys
around a quarter past midnight, as if we have no need
to be here. And somehow the river
is no longer too wet, or too slow, each member of
the expedition has already fallen
into depths of an unfamiliar reflection,
and we are sitting on a cold seat, en route, in our cars.

Nothing Human Is That Perfect

There are no holes of oblivion—what with
spring thickening, our remarkable breath, fingers.
Each defeated horizon is speckled
with survivors who walk away from a final
solution in a final snowfall that can't
possibly be there, but the matter
is not what moves them.

Just as your apartment, with its maroon rugs,
dwarfs the city, a meadow
that slowly fills with light poses no greater
threat than dawn, until the muffled, afternoon fuzziness
favors a stand of willows near the river
and you can't let go of them as they come
to mean something, something more than
feeling the kitchen is haunted after a knife has cut
through an orange, and rests, for an instant,
on the flesh of your hand.

Oh, to need both privacies, alternately,
all the thinking and the lavish
architecture we build up around safety, as if
experience were a commodity to seek out
and protect. If we can trust those rooftops, adrift
among waves of fog or haze, then we can be
strong enough to help without knowing it
this weary procession of passers-by. We can hear
a little girl's story, an accordion player's shaky waltz
that unbends in the leg of each step.

Anxious Latitudes

Up here, I am hyperactively farsighted.
My brain weighs three pounds and
when the show got on the road
my body was a mere appendage of it.

On a clear day, I'm busy directing landscapes,
not really shoving the shrubs around,
not ordering pastel houses from the hillsides,
but carrying them with me like a frayed

photograph in my wallet, so that I might read it
as a small corner of its vaster itinerary.
How the background shows through, blank smudges
and the so many time-connecting dots,

with all I've come to expect deferred to some
higher order, place or pocket watch ticking together,
both of this world and on that side of the fence.
By now, judging from here,

the rewards must be enormous. Though
my body weighs as much as fifty brains,
always doing, always feeling, mostly feeling
(to get gushy), the traffic bangs and

snarls around me, and the collapsed pause
absents all passing scenery before it moves on,
now farther away. This happens every yesterday
and pained expressions linger on our faces.

We can be thankful for that, each one dying
to talk with somebody, just the two of us
bringing it all home, putting together
the movable parts on their merry way.

But time is short, only twenty minutes (we have
the sandwiches to eat) until the loudest voice
coheres as many, lacquering the politics
of company policy, and its words greet us

not with love, but from fear
that repeated toil simply hardens the argument
that work is all there is, like the whistle
signaling a return to designated places.

So when the pay checks are spooned out, I'll take mine
as if to tell you, "O.K., you're right!
You're the victor, now write the history, please."
You see, I don't even know what clothes

I'm wearing, whether or not they are comfortable
or stylish. Just too nervous to care
and I'm on an extended vacation,
sweating in the balance.

About the Author

Ralph Angel was born in Seattle in 1951. He received his B.A. from the University of Washington. Since 1976, he has lived in and around Los Angeles, California. He earned an M.F.A. from the University of California, Irvine, and has taught there and at The California Institute of the Arts. He is currently an assistant professor at the University of Redlands. *Anxious Latitudes* is his first collection of poetry.

About the Book

This book has been composed in Galliard by Graphic Composition of Athens, Georgia. It has been printed on 60 pound Sebago Antique by Kingsport Press of Kingsport, Tennessee. It has been bound by Kingsport Press of Kingsport, Tennessee. Dust jackets and covers have been printed by Phoenix Color Corporation of Long Island City, New York.